Upcycle with Sizzix®

TECHNIQUES AND IDEAS FOR USING DIE-CUTTING AND EMBOSSING MACHINES

Creative Publishing
international

Ellison®

ELLISON EDUCATIONAL
EQUIPMENT, INC.
25862 COMMERCENTRE
DRIVE
LAKE FOREST, CA 92630
sizzix.com
sizzix.co.uk
Ellison® & Sizzix®
are trademarks of
Ellison Educational
Equipment, Inc.
©2014 Ellison

Customer Service Hours
6:30 a.m. to 4:00 p.m.,
Pacific Time,
Monday through Friday

By Phone
877.355.4766
(Toll Free in the USA)
949.598.8821
(Outside of the USA)

CW PRESS

215 Historic 25th Street,
Ogden Utah

First published in the
United States of America in 2015
by Creative Publishing international,
a member of
Quarto Publishing Group USA Inc.
400 1st Ave. No.
Minneapolis, MN 55401
Telephone: 1-800-328-3895
www.creativepub.com

10 9 8 7 6 5 4 3 2 1
ISBN:978-1-58923-883-1

Design Production: Lisa Ballard

Photographer: Ryne Hazen, Hazen Photography

Copy Editor: Cynthia Levens

Kristin HIGHBERG

FOREWORD

People always wonder where we get all the inspiration for our next great creative book... and the answer, of course, is everywhere!

From the corners of a darkened garage to the treasures unearthed at thrift stores and flea markets across the ocean or around the block, inspiration is all around us...sometimes we just have to search for it!

In *Upcycle with Sizzix*, our design team's hunt for the rare, the retro, and the unusual have paid off with an amazing array of repurposed projects to personalize any life. Whether it's fashion, home décor, gift giving, or entertaining, you won't believe how giving an item a second chance can enhance your creativity and your perspective. I know I'll never look at a dated or discarded item the same again!

So as you flip through the pages of this book for the first time or the hundredth time, be sure to dream along with us. There's always something new to do and the possibilities are truly endless!

Happy Crafting,

Kristin Highberg

Chief Executive Officer
Ellison/Sizzix

CONTENTS

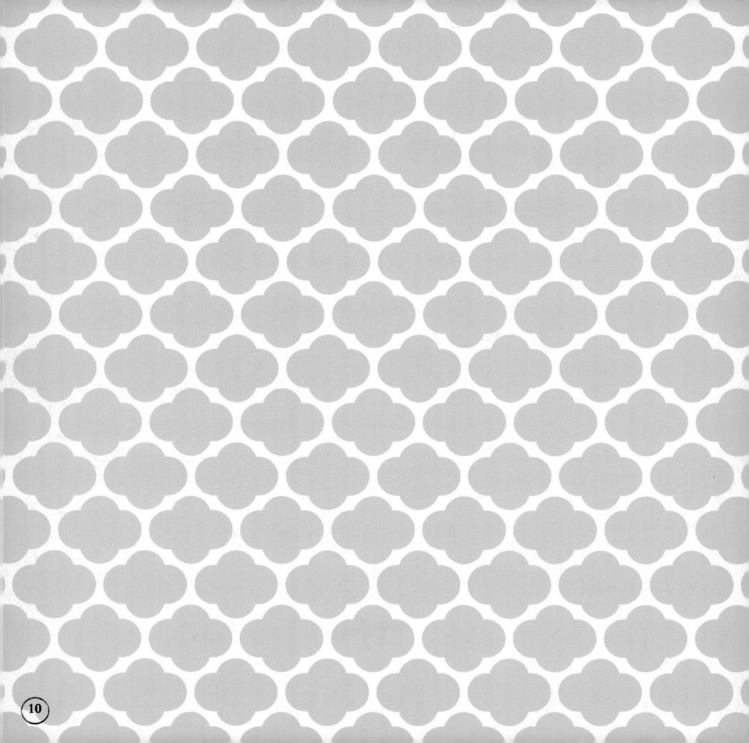

HOW-TO
INSTRUCTIONS

UPCYCLE:

**THE PROCESS OF
CONVERTING OLD
OR DISCARDED
MATERIALS INTO
SOMETHING USEFUL
AND OFTEN
BEAUTIFUL.**

Welcome

TO THE WORLD OF SIZZIX®,

where creativity abounds! Our product line of machines, dies, and accessories delivers unlimited opportunities to create a variety of projects to express your creativity and enhance your life. And while our innovative tools are often associated with paper crafting projects like card making and scrapbooking, they're perfect for making so much more.

This book is full of projects that focus on more. Not only will you see ideas for different types of DIY projects — like fashion and jewelry, home décor, entertaining and gift giving — these projects make use of an incredible variety of upcycled materials. We're sharing ideas that will help you personalize your life in countless ways, while making use of materials and objects that you may never have considered before!

Ideas from the Experts
BEGINNING CRAFTERS WELCOME!

These beautifully upcycled projects have been created by our talented staff crafters, but don't worry — the projects in this book can be embraced by crafters at all levels. Whether you replicate a project exactly, use a particular project as a jumping off place, or just use the volume as ingredients for a future creative recipe, you're sure to find the pages that follow to be an inspirational feast!

Our team worked their magic and transformed items like old lamps, tablecloths, frames, and watchbands into stylish home décor, jewelry organizers, and bracelets. Perfect for you to enjoy or give as gifts, there's a little something for everyone.

LAY OF THE LAND

Rather than taking you through each project step-by-step, *Upcycle with SIZZIX®* is an idea book that will spark your creative fire. Each project photo is accompanied by helpful hints to help you make the project yourself, including the dies used, the upcycled item that was used, and any special notes.

DIE-CUTTING BASICS

Are you new to die cutting and embossing? You're going to love it. Our machines, dies, and embossing folders are easy to use — you'll be hooked! The creative possibilities are truly endless, and talk about a time saver! Why spend ages cutting out 30 paper hearts by hand when making cupcake toppers? You can die-cut them in a minute or two.

You're also going to love the variety of materials you can cut. Our steel rule dies cut materials like fabric, leather, magnetic sheets, burlap, vinyl, foam, felt, compressed sponge, matboard, aluminum cans, and more. If you've never crafted using steel-rule dies, your world of crafting possibilities has just blown wide open!

Getting Started
MAKING A BASIC SIZZIX® SANDWICH USING STEEL RULE DIES

Place a Steel Rule Die on a Cutting Pad with the foam side up. Place paper or desired material to be cut on top of the die. Place the second Cutting Pad on top of the paper or material to create a "sandwich." Slide the sandwich into the opening of the machine. Note the rotation of the handle and continue to rotate it in the same direction until the sandwich has passed through the opening of the rollers. Remove the sandwich from the machine. Your die cut shape is ready to use!

Using Originals™, Bigz™ or other Steel-Rule Dies

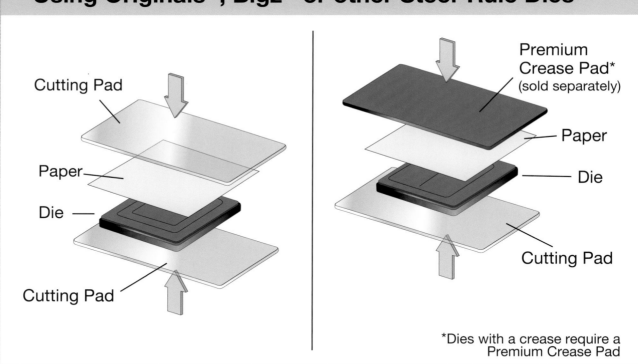

Cutting Pad

Paper

Die

Cutting Pad

Premium Crease Pad*
(sold separately)

Paper

Die

Cutting Pad

*Dies with a crease require a Premium Crease Pad

MACHINES

Big Shot™ | BIGkick™

This versatile die-cutting machine really is the hub of any crafter's universe. As a portable roller machine, it easily cuts and embosses many different materials. Create your own one-of-a-kind cards, invitations, scrapbook pages, home décor, fashion, altered art, quilting and much more!

Big Shot™ Pro

For the crafter who wants it all, comes the pro-strength machine that does it all. From our embossing folders to our smallest dies to our biggest 12" Bigz™ Pro dies, the Big Shot Pro machine works with any Sizzix® die or embossing folder to create an amazing assortment of craft shapes.

Vagabond™

Resembling a well-travelled suitcase on the outside, the Vagabond machine easily opens up to reveal a portable yet powerful machine that takes you to imaginative new places. Upon closer examination, the Vagabond impresses with its uncanny ability to effortlessly cut and emboss many different materials and thicknesses.

Texture Boutique™

Resembling an ornate purse with a beaded handle, this amazing embossing machine is perfect for creating cards for any occasion, transforming ordinary cardstock and other thin materials into elegant embossed art.

SophistiCut™

With a stylish purse design and refined die-cutting capabilities, the SophistiCut creates many charming shapes using small, medium and border-sized Sizzix Originals™ dies. Experience appliqué, home décor, fashion, jewelry, cardmaking and more in pure elegance.

TECHNOLOGY

steel-rule

Look out for Bigz™, Originals™, On The Edge™ and Movers & Shapers™ dies. These will cut a wide range of materials, making them perfect for papercrafting, home décor, quilting and more!

Cuts:
- cardstock
- felt
- fabric
- foam
- magnet
- leather
- craft aluminum
- chipboard
- metallic foil
- and much more!

wafer-thin

Our Framelits™ and Thinlits™ dies are perfect for layering and cutting apertures and a whole host of intricate shapes that will make your papercrafting really stand out from the crowd!

Cuts:
- cardstock
- paper
- metallic foil
- vellum

chemically-etched

Check out our Sizzlits® and Embosslits™. Designed to cut a single sheet of cardstock, Sizzlits create fabulous little shapes that make a great big difference with your papercrafting. Go one step further with Embosslits – these clever little dies cut AND emboss for some very impressive results!

Cuts:
- cardstock
- paper
- metallic foil
- vellum

embossing folders

Our Textured Impressions™ Embossing Folders have male (raised) and female (recessed) surfaces on opposite sides of a folder. When it is passed through a die-cutting or embossing machine, the folder applies pressure to cardstock to alter the surface, giving it a raised effect.

Molded plastic embossing folders do not cut paper. These folders only emboss and are designed to be used with a single sheet of thin material.

quilting/appliqué

This exclusive collection of dies allows you to create personalized quilts and patchwork masterpieces, taking away the sometimes laborious task of using a ruler and rotary cutter. The collection features some of the most popular quilt shapes, including standard squares and triangles, as well as Apple Core, Dresden Plate, Drunkard's Path and much more!

You can cut multiple layers of fabric at any one time with these hardy and versatile dies, giving you a precise and clean cut every time. They even come with a built-in 1/4" seam allowance to make piecing by hand or machine even easier!

TEXTURED IMPRESSIONS

Textured Impressions Embossing Folders offer the deepest and boldest embossing experience. You can turn ordinary cardstock, paper, metallic foil, or vellum into an embossed, textured master-piece. The large folder also fits the exact dimensions of an A2 or A6 card, while the small, medium, or border sizes create amazing embellishments.

ACCESSORIES

Our complete line of accessories will further enhance your creative life. Make creating easier with our Magnetic Platform, Stamper's Secret Weapon, and Tool Kit. Embrace efficiency by using our Cut & Emboss Paper and Mat Board Packs. Expand your creative potential with Embossing Diffusers and the Dimensional Cutting Pad. And don't forget to keep your crafting tools organized with our Die & Embossing Storage!

SYSTEM COMPARISON/COMPATIBILITY CHART

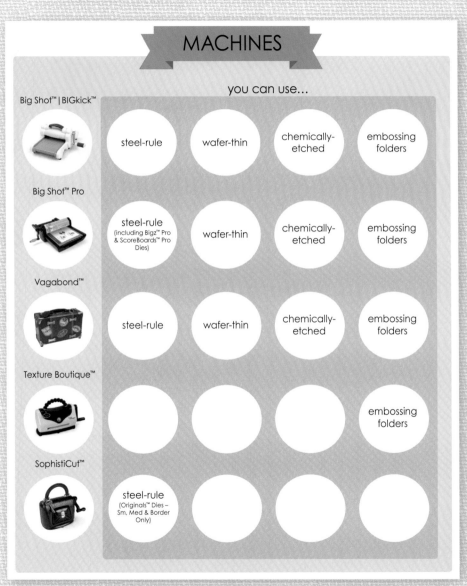

MACHINES

you can use...

	steel-rule	wafer-thin	chemically-etched	embossing folders
Big Shot™ | BIGkick™	steel-rule	wafer-thin	chemically-etched	embossing folders
Big Shot™ Pro	steel-rule (including Bigz™ Pro & ScoreBoards™ Pro Dies)	wafer-thin	chemically-etched	embossing folders
Vagabond™	steel-rule	wafer-thin	chemically-etched	embossing folders
Texture Boutique™				embossing folders
SophistiCut™	steel-rule (Originals™ Dies – Sm, Med & Border Only)			

HOME DÉCOR

It's YOUR DAY!

"Enjoy" BANNER

DIES USED:
Word Play Alphabet, Match Box

RECYCLED ITEMS:
Corrugated packing paper, Wrapping paper scraps

NOTE:
Gently remove the top layer of paper from packaging or old shipping boxes to reveal the corrugated texture.

"Blessings in Stone"

WALL ART

DIE USED:
Word Play Alphabet

RECYCLED ITEM:
Painted canvas mat

NOTE:
Cover sections of mat board with foil, paint entire surface with Distress Paint by Tim Holtz.

"Enjoy the Journey" CLIPBOARD

DIES USED:
3-D Flower,
Leaves,
Stacked Artful Words

RECYCLED ITEM:
Old clipboard

NOTE:
Mixing artificial greenery and twigs with paper die cuts will give the entire project a more realistic look.

"Have a Big Life" PHOTO HOLDER BOOK

DIES USED:
Phrase, Inspire, Leaves

RECYCLED ITEM:
Old book

NOTE:
Before folding the pages of the book, ink the edges with a contrasting color to add depth and dimension.

Succulent
PLANT

DIE USED:
Tattered Pinecone

RECYCLED ITEM:
Miniature silver-plate
water pitcher

NOTE:
Add small dabs of paint
around edges of die cut
leaves for a more
realistic look.

Tattered Florals
CANDLEHOLDER

DIE USED:
Tattered Florals

RECYCLED ITEMS:
Door moulding, Book pages, Leather, Glass insulator

NOTE:
Repeating die cuts in a pattern can create a visually interesting background. The same technique can be applied to walls and furniture.

"Wish" BANNER

DIES USED:
Sassy Serif Alphabet,
Banner

RECYCLED ITEM:
Canvas mat

NOTE:
Applying iron-on
adhesive to your fabric
before die cutting
provides an easy way to
adhere the letters to
the banner.

Floral
SCALLOPED
MIRROR

DIE USED:
Tattered Florals

RECYCLED ITEM:
Denim (for flowers)

NOTE:
Add a light layer of Plaster of Paris to die cut and assembled denim petals to create a ceramic-type flower.

DIE USED:
Tattered Florals Leaves

RECYCLED ITEM:
Lamp

NOTE:
Before die cutting apply
Modge Podge to burlap
and allow to dry to
prevent fabric from
fraying while cutting
and assembling flower.

Daisy-Topped
OIL CAN

DIE USED:
Tattered Florals

RECYCLED ITEM:
Oil can

NOTE:
Apply foil sticker paper to chipboard before die cutting to create a more durable/bendable flower.

Floral LAMPSHADE

DIES USED:
Flowers & Leaves,
Flowers Cottage Trio,
Garden Greens

RECYCLED ITEM:
Lampshade

NOTE:
Apply the die cuts to the
inside of the shade to
create silhouettes when
the light is turned on.

Gold-Foiled CANDLE HOLDERS/VASES

DIES USED:
Honeycomb,
Flower

RECYCLED ITEMS:
Old vases

NOTE:
Apply adhesive to both sides of a piece of paper, die cut the shape, adhere the shape to vase, apply gold foil.

Stenciled CANDLE HOLDER

DIE USED:
Curly Gate

RECYCLED ITEM:
Glass vase

NOTE:
Adhere stencil, spritz glass vase with water, spray Krylon Looking Glass Spray Paint over water, dab glass with a paper towel to create a mercury glass finish.

"*Love*"
PHOTO HOLDER
BOOK

DIES USED:
Flourish, Beautiful Serif
Essentials Alphabet,
Heart

RECYCLED ITEM:
Vintage book

NOTE:
Make your own glitter
paper by running your
paper through a Xyron
adhesive machine.
Peel away the protective
backing to expose the
adhesive, apply
the glitter.

"All You Need is Love"
WALL ART

DIES USED:
Olivia Shapes
& Background,
Edges Alphabet

RECYCLED ITEMS:
Vintage yardsticks

NOTE:
Glue yardsticks, wash
with diluted paint,
temporarily adhere cut
letters, dry-brush acrylic
paint over cut letter,
remove letters.

"Color Outside the Lines"
WALL ART

DIES USED:
Word Play Alphabet,
Block Talk Alphabet

RECYCLED ITEM:
Painted canvas

NOTE:
Attaching the letters
backward on the canvas
gives the illusion of old
type press letters.

Numbered

SMALL CHEST OF DRAWERS

DIE USED:
Cargo Numbers Stencil

RECYCLED ITEM:
Small chest of drawers

NOTE:
Apply repositionable adhesive to paper to create the stencils for the numbers.

Metallic JEWELRY BOX

DIE USED:
Vintage Doily

RECYCLED ITEM:
Domino board game box

NOTE:
Paint domino box with metallic paint. Die cut doily from painted box, adhere to wood box top, finish painting.

"Be You-Tiful"
JEWELRY HOLDER

DIES USED:
Daisy Flowers,
Leaves,
Berry with Branch

RECYCLED ITEMS:
Clipboard,
Plastic packaging
(for flowers)

NOTE:
Die cut thin daisies from
plastic, then spray paint
the daisies. Embellish
with jewels.

Quilted Pocket
CHALKBOARD

DIES USED:
Square Framelits, Heart

RECYCLED ITEM:
Clearance aisle décor

NOTE:
This heart-on-square design would also make a great quilt.

Die Cut Felt
GARLAND

DIE USED:
Flower Layers

RECYCLED ITEMS:
Salvaged lace, Felt

NOTE:
Sew die cut felt shapes onto a strip of vintage lace. Add vintage buttons for decoration.

Family
ORNAMENT

DIES USED:
Bow Tie,
Vintage Market

RECYCLED ITEM:
Old packaging from
craft project

NOTE:
Save your packaging and
paper scraps from other
projects to die cut small
letters and designs.

"Home" FABRIC BANNER

DIE USED:
Banners

RECYCLED ITEM:
Vintage tablecloth

NOTE:
Liquid Stitch may be used as an alternative to machine-stitching the banner.

Tablecloth PILLOW

DIE USED:
Borders & Hydrangea

RECYCLED ITEM:
Tablecloth

NOTE:
For flower, die cut multiple layers of fabric at once to save time.

Embossed Foil
FRAME

DIES USED:
Nouveau Butterfly,
Asian Dragonfly,
Iron Scrollwork

RECYCLED ITEM:
Old photo frame

NOTE:
Use patina inks to add
color to the embossed
metal. Use sandpaper to
sand off some of the
color to expose the
metal color.

I love you because . . .

You make me

Laugh! 😄

"I Love You Because ..."
DRY ERASE BOARD

DIES USED:
Tattered Florals,
Elegant Flourishes

RECYCLED ITEM:
Old photo frame

NOTE:
Change the sentiment
and dry erase pen color
to suit the seasons.

"When This You See" EMBELLISHED VINTAGE BOOK

DIE USED:
Tattered Florals

RECYCLED ITEM:
Vintage book

NOTE:
If you can't find the perfect color or fabric for flowers, you can color cotton organdy with diluted paint or distress inks.

Wooden Spool
PHOTO HOLDER

DIE USED:
Hearts Primitive #3

RECYCLED ITEMS:
Vintage wooden spools,
Felt from old Christmas
stocking

NOTE:
Bind several spools
together with ribbon,
attach photo and die cut
hearts with wire.

ACCESSORIES

Cereal Box
JEWELRY DRESSER

DIES USED:
Matchbox Ornate,
On the Edge,
Scalloped Square

RECYCLED ITEMS:
Cereal boxes

NOTE:
Select a cardboard box
whose inside dimensions
will fit a row of drawers
evenly. Make drawers
from old cereal boxes
using Matchbox Ornate
Die. Add dimension to
the edges of the drawers
by using a distress
rubber stamp ink.

Pincushion
RING HOLDER

DIE USED:
Camelia Flower

RECYCLED ITEMS:
Sauce jar,
Old jewelry beads

NOTE:
Fill the jar with
other jewelry or
jewelry cleaner.

Vintage Frame
JEWELRY ORGANIZER

DIE USED:
Borders

RECYCLED ITEM:
Frame

NOTE:
Make certain to use a
strong enough fabric or
lace and paper to hold
your jewelry. Here
Grunge Paper was used.

Flower
NECKLACE

DIES USED:
Flower,
Flourish

RECYCLED ITEMS:
Old leather purse,
Necklaces, Bracelets,
Earrings

NOTE:
Add dimension to the
edges of the leather
flower by using rubber
stamp ink.

Leather Belt
HEADBAND

DIES USED:
Bird,
Flower,
Leaf

RECYCLED ITEM:
Leather belt

NOTE:
Use purchased ruffled elastic in-between the two ends of the belt to size headband.

"At the Inkwell"
SPOOL NECKLACE

DIE USED:
Writing Desk

RECYCLED ITEM:
Thread spool

NOTES:
Charm die cuts are made from shrink plastic and colored with permanent markers.

Rose WATCHBAND BRACELET

DIE USED:
3-D Flower

RECYCLED ITEMS:
Man's watchband,
Suede jacket

NOTE:
Use a clear drying
adhesive like E6000 to
assemble the 3-D flower.
It can also be used to
attach the flower to the
watchband.

Bangle
BRACELET

DIES USED:
Mini Heart,
Shield

RECYCLED ITEM:
Water bottle

NOTE:
Large water bottles
work best for sizing, the
thicker the water bottle
plastic the better the
bracelet will hold
its shape.

Embossed Metal
TILE PENDANTS

DIE USED:
Texture Fade Circles

RECYCLED ITEMS:
Aluminum cans

NOTE:
Color embossed aluminum with patina inks or alcohol inks.

Cork EARRINGS & NECKLACE

DIE USED:
Flower & Phrases

RECYCLED ITEMS:
Wine corks

NOTE:
Slice wafer thin pieces of wine corks and attach die cuts. Add Epoxy topcoat.

Denim Cuff **BRACELET**

DIE USED:
3-D Rose

RECYCLED ITEM:
Levi jeans

NOTE:
Cut bracelet from waistband of jeans, die cut shapes from denim, roll and attach.

Tin Can
BRACELET

DIE USED:
Circle

RECYCLED ITEMS:
Tin cans or
tin round cake boxes

NOTE:
Drill hole in tin.
Vintage beads can be
placed in between tin
circles.

Old T-shirt Flower
NECKLACE

DIE USED:
Flowers

RECYCLED ITEM:
Old T-shirt

NOTE:
Vary the width of the strips you cut from the old T-shirt to add visual interest to the finished necklace.

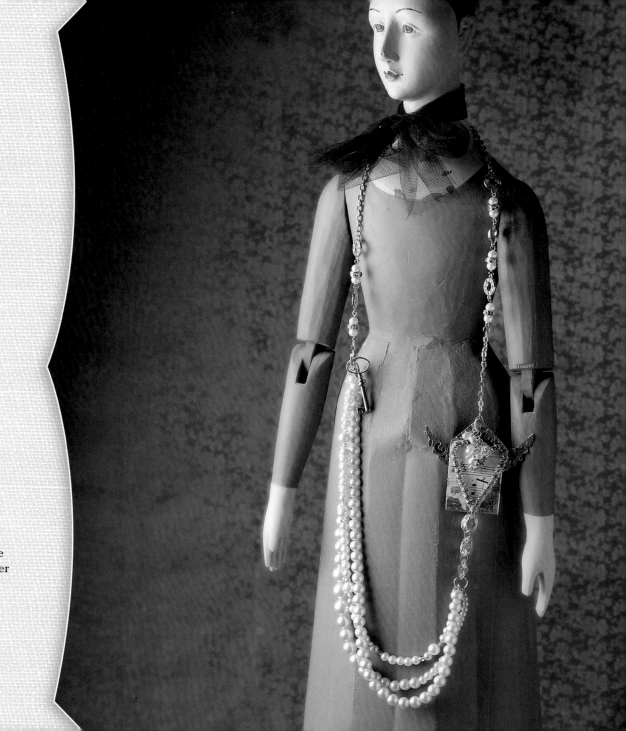

Glitzy
NECKLACE

DIES USED:
Tag,
Heart,
Wing

RECYCLED ITEMS:
Old necklaces

NOTE:
Necklace focal piece
is created from paper
foil covered plastic
packaging.

Eclectic
PURSE

DIES USED:
Bird,
Swirl Case Alphabet

RECYCLED ITEMS:
Pocket from jeans,
Wool for bird from
old jacket,
Old zippers,
Old jewelry

NOTE:
This purse was created by
using left-over elements
from discarded apparel:
decorative pockets were
cut off old jeans to add
embellishments that
did not have to be
hand-made or hand
embroidered, old
zippers were used as the
handles, and jeweled
embellishments are old
pieces of broken jewelry.

Scarf PIN

DIE USED:
Tattered Florals

RECYCLED ITEMS:
Denim jacket,
Felt bag,
Navy button

NOTE:
Die cut denim and felt,
layer, attach to pin.
Embellish with
nautical button from
navy uniform.

Curtain Fabric
POUCH OR WALLET

DIE USED:
Long Card Pro

RECYCLED ITEM:
Salvaged vintage
curtain fabric

NOTE:
Layer fabric with batting
and interfacing, die cut
using a card or envelope.
Stitch up the sides,
embellish with a button
or snap.

Embellished
OMBRE BAG

DIES USED:
Flowers,
Leaves,
Circles,
Ovals

RECYCLED ITEMS:
Children's dresses

NOTE:
Place a row of assorted die cut fabric shapes and ribbon scraps in a line on a piece of paper, sew together, continue until strip is long enough. Tear away paper. You can make your own ombre bag by dipping a plain bag in a bowl of desired color die.

Flower Pin
SHOES

DIES USED:
Bow,
Layered Flower

RECYCLED ITEM:
Shoes

NOTE:
Attach die cuts to shoe clips so they can be changed for different outfits.

Cream Flower
PURSE

DIE USED:
Lilac Flower

RECYCLED ITEM:
Purse

NOTE:
Attach leather flower
pieces with brads.

Leather BELT

DIES USED:
Flower,
Daisy

RECYCLED ITEMS:
Stretch belt,
Leather jacket

NOTE:
Use E600 glue for
adhering jewels.

Vintage HAT

DIE USED:
Tattered Florals

RECYCLED ITEM:
Hat

NOTE:
Create a simplified
version using tissue
paper for the flowers.
This would be a great
party craft.

Fabric Flower
BUTTONS

DIE USED:
Circle

RECYCLED ITEM:
Old jacket

NOTE:
Die cut circles. With circle pieces together inside out, stitch around ¾ of circle, turn, stuff, finish stitching. Create flower by bringing thread up through center of circle, wrap around stuffed circle to underside, insert needle, push needle up through top side of circle, pull thread tight, repeat at intervals. When finished put bead on thread, go back through center, knot.

Old Shirt
I-PAD SLEEVE

DIES USED:
Flourish,
Hand,
Heart,
Vine,
Scrollwork Frame,
Keys,
Tags

RECYCLED ITEMS:
Old shirt,
Salvaged vintage felt

NOTE:
Adhere especially thin
or flimsy fabric to card-
stock before die cutting
to achieve a clean cut.

GIFT GIVING

Vintage Book
PAPER LUMINARY

DIES USED:
Hearts,
Tattered Pinecone

RECYCLED ITEMS:
Vintage book paper,
Food jar

NOTE:
This is a perfect gift for
a book lover.

Bird Branch & Log
GIFT WRAPPING

DIE USED:
Bird & Leaves Texture
Folder

RECYCLED ITEM:
Toilet paper roll

NOTE:
Roll a small gift in tissue
paper. Snip ends of
tissue paper with
multi-bladed scissors,
insert gift into tube.

Matchbox
GIFT BOX

DIES USED:
Lacy Butterfly,
Flourish,
Lacy Heart

RECYCLED ITEMS:
Large matchbox,
Broken Christmas
decoration,
Leftover fabric

NOTE:
Flourish and Lacy Heart
dies were used to make
the stencils on the top of
the matchbox.

Embellished CLIPBOARD

DIES USED:
Word Play,
Caged Bird

RECYCLED ITEM:
Old sheet music

NOTE:
Add a layer of
decoupage to the top
of the clipboard to
secure the paper.

GIFT BOX WITH
Vintage Button

DIE USED:
Bag with Flap

RECYCLED ITEMS:
Torn gift box, Vintage button

NOTE:
Stamp a background onto the bag with white ink before assembling the box.

Leather Leaf
GIFT BOX

DIE USED:
Leaf

RECYCLED ITEM:
Old piece of leather

NOTE:
Attach leaf (shown here out of leather) to elastic. This will allow the decoration to be recycled to another gift box. This is referred to as, "pay it forward recycling!"

Vintage Map
GIFT BOX

DIES USED:
Pinwheel,
Block Talk Alphabet

RECYCLED ITEMS:
Maps,
Brown paper bags

NOTE:
Attach an old map to
chipboard before die
cutting the letters to
add dimension.

By the Sea
MINI ALBUM

DIES USED:
Tag (for pocket pages),
Seahorse,
Sand Dollar

RECYCLED ITEMS:
Toilet paper rolls
(paper towel rolls
can be substituted)

NOTE:
Press paper rolls flat,
then run them through
the die cutting machine
between cutting pads to
completely flatten rolls.

"You've Been Tagged" JAR

DIE USED:
Doily Butterfly

RECYCLED ITEM:
Plastic food bottle

NOTE:
Use wax paper between the die and paper for especially intricate dies. This will help the die cut release from the die more easily.

Gift TAGS

DIE USED:
Tags

RECYCLED ITEMS:
Greeting cards

NOTE:
Rubber stamps are
a perfect way to add
sentiments to any
gift tag.

Egg Carton
GIFT BOX

DIE USED:
Flower

RECYCLED ITEM:
Egg carton

NOTE:
Cut several layers of tissue paper at a time. Staple them together, fluff and separate the layers to create the pompom.

Cookie
CONTAINER

DIE USED:
Bow

RECYCLED ITEMS:
Plastic water bottles

NOTE:
Cut the neck off of two
bottles, cut bottles in
half lengthwise, place
cookies inside.

"Game On"
GIFT BOXES

DIES USED:
ScoreBoards
Block/Cubes 3-D,
Circles

RECYCLED ITEMS:
Game boards

NOTE:
Remember, you can use
the positive or negative
space from your die cuts.

Paper Clip BOOKMARKS

DIE USED:
Prize Ribbon Circle
(Any small shape die
would work)

RECYCLED ITEMS:
Various old food
packaging (candy boxes,
fast food drink cups)

NOTE:
These make great
incentive gifts from
teachers to students or
an inexpensive set of
gifts for your child's
entire class.

Melted Shopping Bag BOX

DIE USED:
Pizza Box

RECYCLED ITEM:
Shopping bags

NOTE:
Flatten several layers of shopping bags between parchment paper, iron to melt. Remove parchment paper, die cut melted bags.

*Sweater*HAT

DIE USED:
Camellia Flower

RECYCLED ITEM:
Button-up sweater

NOTE:
Cut out hat from a
button-up sweater.

Jewelry CARDS

DIE USED:
Jar Labels

RECYCLED ITEMS:
Used gift boxes

NOTE:
If you are out of old gift boxes, try using the chipboard back from a pad of paper (most steno and legal pads have heavy backing).

Soda Box
PARTY FAVORS

DIES USED:
Pillow Box,
Stars

RECYCLED ITEMS:
Soda can boxes

NOTE:
Die cut the pillow box
from the plain section
and the stars from the
printed section of the
soda boxes.

Rose PENCIL

DIE USED:
Heart #3

RECYCLED ITEM:
Felt jacket

NOTE:
Cut hearts from felt.
Glue a "heart petal"
to the end of a pencil,
continue layering
"heart petals" down the
pencil. Tie a ribbon
bow to cover the end.

Embellished
SEWING GIFT TIN

DIES USED:
Scallop Heart Framelits

RECYCLED ITEM:
Mint tin

NOTE:
Match the theme of the gift to the decorations on the tin to create a gift box as well as a container.

Map
STATIONARY

DIES USED:
Scallop on the Edge,
Heart

RECYCLED ITEMS:
Maps

NOTE:
Print personalized
stationary and decorate
with maps before you
die cut.

Vintage Thread
SPOOLS

DIES USED:
Circles,
Heart,
Banner,
Retro Camera Icon

RECYCLED ITEMS:
Vintage thread spools,
Vintage buttons

NOTE:
Hide a dowel rod in
the center of a stack of
vintage spools to create
a tower of spools.

Man's Tie
EYEGLASS CASE

DIES USED:
Scallop Edge,
Heart

RECYCLED ITEMS:
Man's tie,
Wool jacket

NOTE:
Fold and sew a man's
tie to create the pocket.
Die cut a scallop strip of
wool from an old jacket
to embellish the case.

DIE USED:
Bow Tie

RECYCLED ITEMS:
Newspaper,
Old jeans

NOTE:
Adhere decorative
fabric to paper before
die cutting. It makes it
easy to see the crease
lines to fold the bow tie.

Egg Carton
SACHET

DIE USED:
Heart

RECYCLED ITEM:
Egg carton

NOTE:
Die cut egg carton,
stitch three-fourths of
edge, fill with lavender,
complete stitching.

Sewing Kit
IN A JAR

DIES USED:
Camellia,
Sewing Room

RECYCLED ITEM:
Sewing pattern paper

NOTE:
If you want the same
look but don't have
old sewing patterns,
you can always rubber
stamp a pattern onto
tissue paper.

Heart
GIFT BOXES

DIES USED:
Match Box,
Mini Hearts Set

RECYCLED ITEM:
Cardboard box

NOTE:
Use Movers & Shapers
magnetic dies for both
negative and positive
space.

Melted Crayon GIFT TAGS

DIE USED:
Heart

RECYCLED ITEMS:
Old broken crayons

NOTE:
Die cut the heart out of poly foam, stack several layers together to create a mold. Melt the crayons in a melting pot, pour the melted crayon into the poly foam heart mold.

You Melt My Heart
Happy Valentine's D

Fabric Heart
CANDY BAGS

DIE USED:
Heart

RECYCLED ITEM:
Children's cotton dress

NOTE:
Die cut hearts, fill bags with candy, sew hearts onto bags, close bags.

Embellished
JOURNAL

DIES USED:
Flourish,
Hand,
Heart,
Vine,
Scrollwork Frame,
Keys,
Tag

RECYCLED ITEM:
Journal

NOTE:
Adding texture to
cardstock makes such a
great background. Add
rubber stamp ink to the
edges to add dimension.

lovely ideas

Silhouette Embellished
GIFT BOX

DIES USED:
Mini Silhouettes,
Tattered Flower,
Garland

RECYCLED ITEMS:
Die box,
Product packaging

NOTE:
Repurpose packaging
from a SIZZIX® die box
or other product by
covering it with
decorative paper
and adding die cut
embellishments.

Vintage Embroidered Pillowcase TAGS

DIE USED:
Scalloped

RECYCLED ITEM:
Vintage embroidered pillowcase

NOTE:
Die cut fabric and cardstock at the same time, stitch around the edges.

ENTERTAINING

"*Party*" TABLE DECORATION

DIES USED:
Serif Essentials
Alphabet,
Pinwheel

RECYCLED ITEMS:
Coke bottles

NOTE:
Spray-paint empty Coke
bottles to serve as the
container for a party
banner.

Soda Can
NAPKIN RINGS

DIE USED:
Camellia Flower

RECYCLED ITEMS:
Aluminum drink cans

NOTE:
Cover metal napkin rings with a strip of the can to match the flowers.

Jar Lid
REFRIGERATOR
MAGNET

DIES USED:
Doily,
Scalloped Circle

RECYCLED ITEMS:
Jar lid,
Promotional magnet
sheets from retailers

NOTE:
A clothes pin is
adhered behind the lid
with a magnet adhered
to the clothes pin so that
it will stay on a metal
surface. Make a magnet
for each party guest to
take home.

Bottle Caps
WINE GLASS
CHARMS

DIES USED:
Flip Flops,
Label

RECYCLED ITEMS:
Bottle caps

NOTE:
Use permanent markers
to add color and detail
to the shrink plastic
charms before you
shrink them.

Old Sweater SILVERWARE HOLDER

DIE USED:
Pillow Box

RECYCLED ITEM:
Old gray sweater

NOTE:
Adhere paper to sweater pieces before die cutting to add a "lining" color.

Paper Bag
PLACEMAT

DIE USED:
Vintage Lace Edging

RECYCLED ITEM:
Paper bag

NOTE:
If you don't have perfect lettering, print the sentiment on the computer and trace it onto the bag. Go over the traced letters with a metallic pen.

Hello Kitty
PURSE

DIES USED:
Hello Kitty,
"Hello"

RECYCLED ITEMS:
Nesquik container,
Belt

NOTE:
Punch holes in opposite
ends of the belt, cut off
the buckle. Punch holes
in the container, insert
brads through the belt
holes and container.
Secure in place.

Flower
PARTY CUPS

DIE USED:
Daisy Flower

RECYCLED ITEMS:
Vintage party cups

NOTE:
A quick change of die
cut and cup color will
create a completely
different look
(for example, red cups
and an apple die cut
would be great for
school parties).

119

"Thank You" JAR FAVORS

DIES USED:
Framelit Banners,
Scallop Circle

RECYCLED ITEMS:
Baby food jars,
Candy packaging

NOTE:
Use candy packaging to
cut banner flags.

THANK YOU

THANK YOU

THANK YOU

Popcorn Bar
SIGNS

DIE USED:
Ornamental Shape

RECYCLED ITEMS:
Goldfish cracker
packaging,
Corrugated cardboard

NOTE:
Paint signs with chalk-
board paint, and label
them with a chalk pen to
make them reusable.

Soup Can
SILVERWARE CADDY

DIE USED:
Royal Labels

RECYCLED ITEMS:
Soup cans

NOTE:
Use the computer to print the sentiment you want to use, then die cut the sentiment using Royal Labels.

Tin Can
PLANTER

DIES USED:
Tag Collection,
Framelits Primitive Stars

RECYCLED ITEMS:
Tin can,
Wooden food skewers

NOTE:
Cover a tin can with
pretty paper to create a
decorative cover for a
small potted flower.

Add die cuts to wooden
skewers to create flower
picks or personalized
place cards.

Cereal Snack **BOXES FOR KIDS' PARTIES**

DIE USED:
Box #3

RECYCLED ITEM:
Cereal box

NOTE:
For children's parties, make small boxes and fill them with their "matching cereal" for the kids to snack on before the party lunch.

Salt Shaker
PARTY PLACE CARDS

DIE USED:
Textured Impressions
Jar Labels

RECYCLED ITEMS:
Old ledger paper,
Salt & pepper shakers

NOTE:
Cut the ends off of large
safety pins, use the
pins to secure cards in
vintage salt and pepper
shakers.

Table Seating
ASSIGNMENTS

DIE USED:
Label

RECYCLED ITEMS:
Slide holders

NOTE:
Seating assignment
cards can be used at
weddings or parties.
Create custom business
cards, display them in
slide holders.

Dress Shirt
WINE BAG

DIE USED:
Feather

RECYCLED ITEMS:
Postcard,
Man's dress shirt

NOTE:
Cut off arm from a
dress shirt, stitch or
glue the bottom to
form the bag.

Die cut a feather from
an old postcard.

Candle Holder
CAKE STAND

DIES USED:
Decorative Strip Lace,
Victorian

RECYCLED ITEMS:
Pedestal candle holder,
Plate

NOTE:
Thin dies like
Decorative Strip Lace
will cut fun foam with
ease. Painting the foam
the same color as the
cake stand makes it look
complete.

Brown Paper
RECIPE BOX

DIES USED:
Banners,
Word Play,
Match Box,
Eat & Taste

RECYCLED ITEMS:
Brown paper
gift box

NOTE:
Give each guest at the
dinner party a copy
of your favorite recipe
served that evening.

Vintage Bottle
PLACE CARDS

DIE USED:
Sign

RECYCLED ITEMS:
Old photos,
Old bottles

NOTE:
Die cut photos of guests
to add on top of old
bottles.

Recipe
Gift Box
PARTY FAVORS

DIES USED:
Box Long,
Medallion
Layering Hearts

RECYCLED ITEM:
Old cookbook

NOTE:
Line up paper so a short
recipe fits on the top of
the box.

Tin Can VASES

DIES USED:
Celebrate,
Tags with Fruit Holes,
Love Hearts & Border,
Hello Summer,
Winged Beauties

RECYCLED ITEMS:
Food cans,
Leather garment

NOTE:
Tying the leather onto
the cans with ribbon
makes it easy to change
them out for different
holidays or events.

Frost-Stenciled
VOTIVE

DIE USED:
Heart

RECYCLED ITEM:
Salad dressing jar

NOTE:
Use die cuts as a mask,
and then spray jar with
frosted spray.

Match Box
PARTY FAVORS

DIES USED:
Match Box,
Star,
Banner,
Flourish

RECYCLED ITEM:
Shoe box

NOTE:
Cut multiples of each
shape and store in a bag.
Then you have them on
hand when you need a
quick gift box.

Picture Frame
SERVING TRAY

DIES USED:
Frameworks,
Courtyard

RECYCLED ITEMS:
Picture frame,
Maps

NOTE:
Using a frame as the
tray allows you to
change out the design
when you want a
new look.

Circus Party
TABLE
DECORATION

DIES USED:
Clown,
Lion,
Under the Big Top,
Rosette

RECYCLED ITEM:
Animal cracker box

NOTE:
Attach paper figures to
colored straws, insert
them into a foam base
inside the box. Cover
buttons to create the
wagon wheels.

Drink Holder
BUFFET CADDY

DIE USED:
Spooky Crows & Cat

RECYCLED ITEM:
Fast food drink caddy

NOTE:
Seasonal dies can be used to decorate caddies for each holiday.

Christmas
Card
SERVING PLATE

DIES USED:
Christmas Ornament,
Snowflake

RECYCLED ITEMS:
Old Christmas cards,
Glass plate

NOTE:
To make sure the
die cuts stay on
permanently, paint
with decoupage, or if
you want to change the
design often, adhere
the die cuts with
removeable adhesive.

DRINKING STRAW
Heart Decorations

DIE USED:
Heart

RECYCLED ITEM:
Vintage stationery

NOTE:
This is also a great way to make your own party picks for cupcakes or appetizers. Just replace straws with picks or skewers.

The Artists ....

Debi ADAMS

Debi Adams has been in the crafting industry for nearly, well, we would date her if we said just how long! Let's just say she's been crafting as long as she can remember. She has experience in sewing, floral arranging, wall murals, home décor, and event planning (especially weddings) as well as cardmaking, scrapbooking, and crafting in general. Debi has been featured in *Somerset Studio*, *Apronology*, and *Creating Keepsakes* magazines as well as a variety of other publications.

She considers herself blessed to have worked with many licensed designers in the art industry such as Tim Holtz and Brenda Walton. Her hobbies include junking, repurposing, and traveling. Having raised four daughters, Debi is now an empty nester and relishes time with her girls when they are in town!

To find out more about Debi visit, www.doodlesinmysketchpad. blogspot.com

Wendy CUSKEY

Wendy has been scrapbooking for over 10 years and enjoys creating mini albums as unique gifts and to showcase summer beach days and the family vacations she enjoys with her husband, two boys, and her yorkie. After working in the legal field for over 20 years, Wendy has transitioned into her job here at SIZZIX® and knows she is truly blessed to have found employment where she can practice her passion each and every day.

Cara has been creating designs for as long as she can remember and currently spends her days working as art director for Ellison. She enjoys spending time with her husband, Glenn and their two kids, Aubrey and Drew. Cara also loves going to the beach, which she is able to do quite often since she lives in warm and sunny Southern California. When she's not planning the next fun event for her kids, her free time is spent taking pictures. She has a passion making fun, inexpensive projects that her friends and family can enjoy.

Cara **MARIANO**

Beth Reames has been in the arts and crafts/scrapbooking industry for 16 years. She has a passion for upcycled, recycled DIY projects. Beth loves the challenge of merging the latest trends in art and home décor with die-cutting and paper crafting. On most weekends you can find her scouring thrift shops, yard sales, and flea markets looking for inspiration and cool junk that she can haul home for her next project.

Beth **REAMES**